JOHN CONSTABLE

Copyright © 1981, Verkerke B.V. All rights reserved.
Produced by V.O.C.-Angel Books, Leidsestraat 12, Amsterdam.
Design: Roon van Santen
Printed in Germany by Mohndruck, Gütersloh
ISBN 90 6560 051 5
V.O.C.-ordernumber 7018

CONSTABLE

JOHN CONSTABLE

V.O.C. - Amsterdam

The Valley of the Stour with Dedham in the distance
(detail)   *c.* 1800-05

I believe I have thought more seriously on my
profession than at any other time of my life – that
is, which is the surest way to real excellence ... For
these two years past I have been running after
pictures and seeking the truth at second hand ... I
am come to a determination to make no idle visits
this summer or to give up my time to common
place people. I shall shortly return to Bergholt
where I shall make some laborious studies from
nature – and I shall endeavour to get a pure and
unaffected representation of the scenes that may
employ me with respect to colour particularly and
any thing else – drawing I am pretty well master of.

*East Bergholt was the village where John Constable
had been born in June 1776. His father, Golding
Constable, owned water mills in Flatford and
Dedham, and a windmill in East Bergholt.*

The Church at East Bergholt   *c.* 1810 - 15

The landscape painter must walk in the fields with a humble mind. No arrogant man was ever permitted to see nature in all her beaty. If I may be allowed to use a solemn quotation, I would say most emphatically to the student, 'Remember now thy Creator in the days of thy youth.'

The rector of the village church was grandfather to Maria Bicknell, Constable's love. He disapproved of the relationship between the son of a country tradesman and his granddaughter, an heiress, and blocked their marriage for some years.

The sound of water escaping from mill dams, ...
willows, old rotten banks, slimy posts, and
brickwork. I love such things – Shakespeare could
make anything poetical ... As long as I do paint I
shall never cease to paint such places. They have
always been my delight ... I should paint my own
places best – Painting is but another word for
feeling. I associate my 'careless boyhood' to all that
lies on the banks of the *Stour*. They made me a
painter (& I am grateful), that is I had often
thought of pictures of them before I had ever
touched a pencil.

Maria Bicknell   1816

I would not be without your portrait for the world.
The sight of it soon calms my spirit under all the
trouble and it is always the first thing I see in the
morning and the last at night.

*This portrait was painted in September 1816, a
month before the couple's eventual wedding at
St.Martins-in-the-Fields in London.*

I am always delighted with the melancholy grandeur
of a sea shore.

*Constable visited Weymouth Bay when he and
Maria were guests at the vicarage in Osmington,
near Weymouth Bay, during part of their
honeymoon. The vicar, John Fisher, was a close
friend and a supporter of Constable.*

Flatford Mill on the River Stour   1816-17
I am now in the midst of a large picture here which
I have contemplated for the next Exhibition – it
would have made my mind easy had it been
forwarder – I cannot help it – we must not expect
to have all our wishes complete.

*Flatford Mill in the background belonged to John
Constable's father.*

I now fear (for my family's sake) I shall never be a
popular artist – a Gentlemen and Ladies painter –
but I am spared making a fool of myself – and your
hand stretched forth teaches me to value my own
natural dignity of mind (if I may say so) above all
things. This is of more consequence than Gentlemen
and Ladies can well imagine as its influence is very
apparent in a painter's work – sometimes the
'éclats' of other artists occasionally cross my mind –
but I look to what I possess and find ample
compensation.

Constable's work was not over-appreciated in Britain. When he was approached by a Paris dealer who wanted to take the Hay Wain over to France, he wrote to Fisher again, asking his advice. John Fisher replied:

Let your Hay Cart go to Paris by all means ... I would (I *think*) let it go at less than its price for the sake of the éclat it may give you. The stupid English public, which has no judgement of its own, will begin to think there is something in you if the French make your works national property.

The picture was a great success in Paris.

Cloud Study (detail)   1822

I have not been Idle and have made more particular
and general study than I have ever done in one
summer ... I have done a good deal of skying – I
am determined to conquer all difficulties and that
most arduous one among the rest – That landscape
painter who does not make his skies a very material
part of his composition – neglects to avail himself
of one of his greatest aids ... The sky is the 'source
of light' in nature – and governs every thing.

Salisbury Cathedral from the Bishop's Grounds 1823
My Cathedral looks very well. Indeed I got through
that job uncommonly well considering how much I
dreaded it. It is much approved by the Academy
and moreover in Seymouth St. though I was at one
time fearful it would not be a favourite there owing
to a *dark cloud* ... It was the most difficult subject
in landscape I ever had upon my easil. I have not
flinched at the work, of the windows, buttresses,
etc., etc., but I have as usual made my escape in the
evanescence of the chiaroscuro.

*Bishop Fisher of Salisbury was an old family friend
and it had been on an earlier visit that Constable
had met his nephew John Fisher.*

*The Bishop's London residence was in Seymour
Street. He disapproved of Constable's liking for
dark, threatening clouds.*

My *friends* all tell me it is my best. Be that as it may, I have done my best. It is a good subject and an admirable instance of the picturesque.

My picture is liked at the Academy. Indeed it forms a decided feature and its light cannot be put out, because it is the light of nature – the Mother of all that is valuable in poetry, painting or anything else – where an appeal to the soul is required ... My execution annoys most of them and all the scholastic ones – perhaps the sacrifices I make for *lightness* and *brightness* is too much, but these things are the essence of landscape.

Brighton is the receptacle of the fashion and
offscourings of London. The magnificence of the
sea, and its ... everlasting voice, is downed in the
din and lost in the tumult of stage coaches ... and
the beach is only Piccadilly ... by the sea-side.
Ladies *dressed* and *undressed* – gentlemen in
morning gowns and slippers on, or without them
altogether about *knee deep* in the breakers –
footmen – children – nursery maids, dog, boys,
fishermen – *preventive service men* (with hangers
and pistols), rotten fish and those hideous
amphibious animals the old bathing women ... all
are mixed up together in endless and indecent
confusion. The genteeler part, the marine parade, is
still more unnatural – with its trimmed and neat
appearance and the dandy jetty or chain pier ...
strides into the sea a full quarter of a mile. In short
there is nothing here for a painter but the breakers
– and the sky – which have been lovely indeed and
always varying.

*Despite his dislike of Brighton society, Constable
often visited the town and painted some of his
finest paintings there. The family used to go
because of Maria's delicate health. She was to die
four years later in 1828, leaving seven children,
ranging in age from eleven months to eleven years.*

The Leaping Horse (detail)   1825

The large subject now on my easel is most
promising and if time allows I shall far excell my
other large pictures in it. It is a canal and full of
the bustle incident to such a scene where four or
five boats are passing with dogs, horses, boys &
men & women & children, and best of all old
timber-props, water plants, willow stumps, sedges,
old nets, *etc., etc., etc.*

After the picture had left for the exhibition,
Constable wrote:

I must say that no one picture ever departed from
my easel with more anxiety on my part with it. It is
a lovely subject, of a canal kind, lively – and
soothing – calm and exhilarating, fresh – and
blowing, but it should have been on my easel a few
weeks longer.

I have dispatched a large landscape to the Academy
– upright, the size of my Lock – but a subject of a
very different nature – inland – cornfields – a close
lane, kind of thing – but it is not neglected in any
part. The trees are more than usually studied and
the extremities well defined – as well as their species
– they are shaken by a pleasant and healthfull
breeze ... My picture occupied me wholly – I could
think of and speak to no one. I was like a friend of
mine in the battle at Waterloo – he said he dared
not turn his head to the right or left – but always
kept it straight forward – thinking of himself alone.

A Watermill at Gillingham

This is a melancholy place – but it is beautiful, full of little bridges, rivulets, mills & cottages – and the most beautiful trees & verdure I ever saw. The poor people are dirty, and to approach one of the cottages is almost insufferable.

Sketch for
Hadleigh Castle   *c.* 1829
At Hadleigh there is the ruin of a castle which from
its situation is a really fine place – it commands a
view of the Kent hills, the Nore and North Foreland
and looking many miles to sea.

There has never been an age, however rude or uncultivated, in which the love of landscape has not in some way been manifested. And how could it be otherwise? for man is the sole intellectual inhabitant of one vast natural landscape. His nature is congenial with the elements of the planet itself, and he cannot but sympathize with its features, its various aspects, and its phenomena in all situations.

Am I doomed never to see the living scenes – which
inspired the landscape of Wilson & Claude
Lorraine? No! but I was born to paint a happier
land, my own dear England – & when I forsake
that, or cease to love my country – may I as
Wordsworth says

    'never more, hear
    Her green leaves rustle
    Or her torrents roar.'

SOURCES

John Constable's Correspondence (JCC), 6 vols.,
edited by R.B. Beckett and published by the Suffolk
Records Society.
Lectures by John Constable, published in 1836.

Letter to John Dunthorne, May 1802 *JCC* II: 31-2
Lectures, 1836, p. 72
1821, *JCC* VI: 7-8
Letter to Maria Bicknell, August 1816, *JCC* II: 195
Letter to Maria Bicknell, July 1814, *JCC* II: 127
Letter to Maria Bicknell, Sept. 1816, *JCC* II: 203
Letter to John Fisher, 1821, *JCC* VI: 63
Letter from John Fisher, 1821, *JCC* VI: 151
Letter to John Fisher, Oct. 1822, *JCC* VI: 76-7
Letter to John Fisher, May 1820, *JCC* VI: 115
Letter to John Fisher, April 1824, *JCC* VI: 155
Letter to John Fisher, May 1824, *JCC* VI: 157
Letter to John Fisher, Aug. 1824, *JCC* VI, 171
Letter to John Fisher, Jan. 1825: *JCC* VI, 198
Letter to John Fisher, April 1826, *JCC* VI: 216-17
Letter to Maria Bicknell, 1827, *JCC* II: 287
Letter to Maria Bicknell, July 1814, *JCC* II: 127
Lectures, 1836, p. 72
Letter to John Fisher, 1823, *JCC* VI: 117

Most of the paintings reproduced in this book are to be found in the Victoria and Albert Museum, London. *The Haywain* and *The Cornfield* are at the National Gallery, London; *The Leaping Horse* is at the Royal *Academy of Arts,* London.